CRUEL SHOES

CRUEL SHOES

by STEVE MARTIN

G. P. PUTNAM'S SONS

New York

Art and design direction by William E. McEuen
Designed by Bernard Schleifer

Photo on page 123 by S. Schwartz;
all other photos by Bobby Klein.

Library of Congress Cataloging in Publication Data

Martin, Steve.
    Cruel shoes.

    I. Title.
PN6162.M259   1978   818'.5'407   78–12473
ISBN 0–399–12304–0
Fifth Impression

PRINTED IN THE UNITED STATES OF AMERICA

To the audience, without whom I would only be myself.

CONTENTS

10

I have spoken of indigestion and garlic!
I have spoken of small round beads!
I tell of years untold in somewhat
starry cities of light! I am telling
of crowned sparrows and ceilings lights
and magnets and flakes and wreckless
winters eating cornflowers!

I am a fish of the sky!
a cloud of the sea!
blue is to fish,
as sky is to me.

YOU ARE walking down a country road. It is a quiet afternoon. You look up and far, far down the road you see someone walking toward you. You are surprised to have noticed someone so far away. But you keep walking, expecting nothing more than a friendly nod as you pass. He gets closer. You see he has bright orange hair. He is closer—a white satin suit spotted with colored dots. Closer—a painted white face and red lips. You and he are fifty yards apart. You, and a full-fledged clown holding a bicycle horn are twenty yards apart. You approach on the lonely country road. You nod. He honks and passes.

MY UNCLE'S METAPHYSICS

MY UNCLE WAS the one who developed and expounded a system of cosmology so unique and unexpected, that it deserves to be written down; his papers were destroyed by fire. I am reconstructing his philosophy from memory as he told it to me on my birthdays and other such holidays. We would be sipping lemonade, perhaps, and he would begin to rock and peer at the sky on those cool afternoons, and with a slow drawl, begin to explain in the cleanest logic why the sky existed, why the universe was the total of all information yet unknown, and how each star in every galaxy could be plotted and predicted in three dimensional space by a three dimensional number system. Then he would explain to me his numerical device called random mathematics, where any equation could be unbalanced for any reason that existed. With it, he predicted to the minute the gestation period of the white giraffe.

As the afternoon rolled on, he fluently spoke philosophy and lost all inhibitions of language, explaining complex ideas with gestures, it seemed. He expressed how sorry he was I had ever heard the word *God*, and then said something about M39. (Later I discovered that this was a method of numbering the galaxies.)

DEMOLITION OF
THE CATHEDRAL AT CHARTRES

Mr. Rivers was raised in the city of New York, had become involved in construction and slowly advanced himself to the level of crane operator for a demolition company. The firm had grown enormously, and he was shipped off to France for a special job. He started work early on a Friday and, due to a poorly drawn map, at six-thirty one morning in February began the demolition of the Cathedral at Chartres.

The first swing of the ball knifed an arc so deadly that it tore down nearly a third of a wall and the glass shattered almost in tones, and it seemed to scream over the noise of the engine as the fuel was pumped in the long neck of the crane that threw the ball through a window of the Cathedral at Chartres.

The aftermath was complex and chaotic, and Rivers was allowed to go home to New York, and he opened up books on the Cathedral and read about it and thought to himself how lucky he was to have seen it before it was destroyed.

THE CONFESSIONS OF
RAYMOND TO HIS GOLDFISH

SOMETIMES I FIND MYSELF gazing away. Often
it's sudden and in the most interesting
company. Then I return to the eyes and the
words traversing the room. But in that
moment of time, the soul of me is exalted
and weeping and gazing, gazing. I'm wor-
ried. Perhaps unconcerned with the most
interesting people, I shall waste away, ne-
glecting to feed you or speak as I pass, or I
shall sit in stoned solace before a picture on
a wall, a picture that has plunged me back
onto a sofa. Fish, to let you know, if I am
ever fixed on a point in space, and your
bowl should sliver or crack and break across
this floor, my mind will see you in slow
motion edging across the table and onto

your downward flight to the ground, I shall stand up and shriek and rush to you and find the water to save you.

THE BORING LEADING
THE BORED

(Reprinted from "Boredom" Magazine)

"WELL, I NEVER!" said Mrs. Watkins. The meeting of the College Council on Metaphysics then applauded her and stood up cheering. Of course, some of the old-school existentialists humbugged it, but nevertheless, the response was overwhelmingly positive. Then Mrs. Jenkins shouted over the crowd, "That woman never ceases to amaze me." The logicians and semanticists gloated and looked anxiously over to the metaphysicians to see their reaction to the carefully planted "never ceases" insertion. Mrs. Jenkins obviously had been working for the logicians to arouse insurrection among the three or four Zeno partisans. But suddenly Dr. Walker, who had been a recluse professor for almost twenty years, stood up. With the crowd instantly silenced by his commanding and unexpected rising, he uttered something so incredibly unutterable, so impossible, so unsolvable, that this mass of philosophy started heaving right and left and dying on the spot, blood bursting from their ears in an astounding death agony.

CRUEL SHOES

ANNA KNEW she had to have some new shoes today, and Carlo had helped her try on every pair in the store. Carlo spoke wearily, "Well, that's every pair of shoes in the place."

"Oh, you must have one more pair. . . ."

"No, not one more pair. . . . Well, we have the cruel shoes, but no one would want . . ."

Anna interrupted, "Oh yes, let me see the cruel shoes!"

Carlo looked incredulous. "No, Anna, you don't understand, you see, the cruel shoes are . . ."

"Get them!"

Carlo disappeared into the back room for a moment, then returned with an ordinary shoebox. He opened the lid and removed a hideous pair of black and white pumps. But these were not an ordinary pair of black and white pumps; both were left feet, one had a right angle turn with separate compartments that pointed the toes in impossible directions. The other shoe was six inches long and was curved inward like a rocking chair with a vise and razor blades to hold the foot in place.

Carlo spoke hesitantly, ". . . Now you see why . . . they're not fit for humans . . ."

"Put them on me."

"But . . ."

"Put them on me!"

Carlo knew all arguments were useless. He knelt down before her and forced the feet into the shoes.

The screams were incredible.

Anna crawled over to the mirror and held her bloody feet up where she could see.

"I like them."

She paid Carlo and crawled out of the store into the street.

Later that day, Carlo was overheard saying to a new customer, "Well, that's every shoe in the place. Unless, of course, you'd like to try the *cruel shoes*."

THE BOHEMIANS

WERE THEY REBELS? Were they artists? Were they outcasts from society? They were all of these. They were The Bohemians.

These bohemians, Mr. and Mrs. Clarence Williams, and their seven children, Biff, Tina, Sparky, Louise, Tuffy, Mickey, and Biff Number Two, lived in a notorious artists' colony and planned community.

Naturally, the bohemians' existence thrived on creativity. Early in the morning, Mrs. Williams would rise and create breakfast. Then, Mr. Williams, inspired by his wife's limitless energy, would rush off to a special room and create tiny hairs in a sink. The children would create things, too. But being temperamental artists, they would often flush them away without a second thought.

But the bohemians' creativity didn't stop there. Mr. Williams would then rush downtown and create reams and reams of papers with numbers on them and send them out to other bohemians who would create special checks to send to him with figures like $7.27 written on them.

At home, the children would be creating unusual music, using only their voices to combine in avant-garde, atonal melodies.

Yes, these were the bohemians. A seething hot-bed of rebellion—the artists, the creators of all things that lie between good and bad.

SERIOUS DOGS

I HAD ALWAYS THOUGHT dogs to be playful and spirited; to me they were animals who loved to chase sticks and romp around and lick you. That is, I *used* to think that, until that day I met the serious dogs. When I first saw the serious dogs, they were sitting on a small hill out to the side of my house watching the sunset. One dog was standing on his hind legs, leaning his elbow on a tree, lost in melancholy thought. They all watched this particularly glorious sunset, then each sighed in turn and strolled in a pack over the hill. Were these the dogs I had thrown bones to for the last several months? These day-dreamers?

Several days later I saw the serious

dogs lunching under the willow. They were not gulping their food down like Spritzie does; they seemed almost refined. After dining they buried their trash, cleaned themselves up, and disappeared over the horizon. I waited about half an hour and then took my shovel over to that willow and dug up what they had buried there: several wrappers of cheese, some half-eaten doggie biscuits, and Good Lord! . . . two empty bottles of fairly expensive Bordeaux! I turned, confused, and saw a small pamphlet lying on the ground. I picked it up and read the title, "Federal Migratory Waterfowl Stamps." "Well," I thought, "some poor stamp collector left his book here . . ." Just then, one of the serious dogs appeared and gently took the volume from my hands and padded off.

I stopped. This was something more than just some dogs who didn't like to play fetch. I decided to secretly follow this dog. I laid about a hundred yards back and watched him. I was impressed with his courtesy to other animals and his compulsion to leave his pathway neat. If a branch had fallen over he would right it; if leaves had blown over this trail, he would brush them back onto less traveled ground.

Then I saw him crawl through an opening in some thick brush. As I approached, I could hear the sounds of other dogs moving lightly. I moved toward the opening and cautiously peered through. I could see a few dogs staring intently at something, as though studying it. I could not make out exactly what it was so I moved in closer. I was sure not to make my presence known. As I parted some branches in the brush, I saw a most incredible sight. A fully-constructed skeleton of a cow! The construction was crude to be sure, but, missing only the head and feet, it was well-formed and highly commendable. I remembered throwing them bones now and then, and I could recall several of the dogs seemingly analyze it before accepting it. I looked along the ground and saw several of my books I had thrown out months before. They were well-kept and stored upright. Most were reference, but I recognized several of the better novels. Then I noticed some dogs all facing

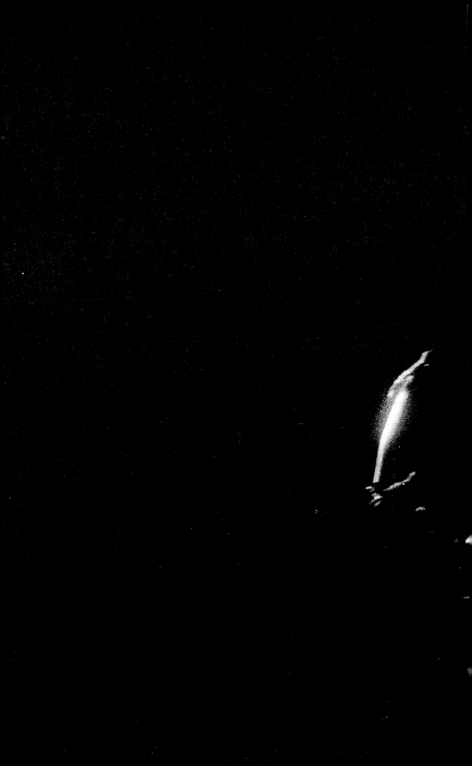

something and sniffing judiciously like connoisseurs would sniff wine. I could not make out what they were looking at as a bush blocked my line of sight. I moved ever so slowly through the underbrush, with such caution that it took me a full ten minutes to travel five feet. Then, with some trepidation, I lifted my eyes at the object of the dogs' curiosity and saw . . . My God! . . . *THE LOST MONET!*

THE STEPHEN MARTIN COLLECTION OF AMERICAN ART: THE MAN BEHIND THE GENIUS

AT THIRTY-THREE, Stephen Martin has formed one of the most extensive collections of nineteenth and early twentieth century American art in existence. It was acquired through elaborate business deals, admitted swindles, and outright cash purchases. Although the collection superbly represents each artist, it maintains a uniqueness only matched by Martin's own unique personality. For example, one particular painting, a Hudson River landscape, signed T. Worthington Whittredge, is in reality a Bierstadt, and Martin claims it to be "an outstanding example of the work of Frederic E. Church, even if it is a Bierstadt."

The collection consists of over one hundred twenty major works: twelve by Thomas Cole, thirteen by Eakins, and an astonishing sixteen by Winslow Homer. Martin has the only genre painting known by Cole, a 24" x 36" study of a cow playing a guitar. Of Eakins, Martin says, "I've included Eakins because I think he was good. I know some will say his presence mars the collection, but I believe time will vindicate me, and Eakins will achieve the status of a J. Peptides or a Madelyn Moons." And as for Homer, "Some of his watercolors were doomed to the fireplace during the winter months of the fuel crisis, but, I am pleased to say, they gave off a vivid glow characteristic of Homer." When asked if he was forced to burn any Homer oils, Martin looked indignant. "Never!" he insisted.

The collection was to be shown at the Metropolitan in the winter of this year, but Martin withdrew the offer suddenly. "These paintings were never meant to be shown during daylight saving time. These pictures deserve more than the false viewing hours dictated by a light-saving gimmick." Thus the collection may not be seen until perhaps nineteen eighty-six, and then only with Martin's peculiar stipulation that they be hung not according to artist or period, but by weight, with classifications of lightweights, middleweights, and heavyweights. Martin is convinced that weight and smell are the only proper study of pictures and all too often is the nose ignored in evaluating works of art. He often takes a picture in hand and hefts it about, then smells every segment of the canvas.

A sense of humor about his collection is Martin's most likable quality. Not free from the pitfall that plagues all art collectors—fakes—Martin discovered one of his Primitives, supposedly painted in seventeen sixty-five, was not all it was supposed to be. Martin pointed it out himself when he noticed the sitter was wearing a Seiko watch. Martin's response was typical: "Well, all the more primitive!"

On another occasion, after a long and tiring negotiation wherein he acquired a delightful 9″ x 14″ drawing by Robert Henri, he approached the work with a jar of solvent and began to rub, revealing a 19″ x 24″

oil by Eastman Johnson hidden beneath. Martin was subsequently sued, the prosecution saying he knew the more valuable painting was there all along. Martin won the case, arguing that his actions were completely spontaneous, and proved his point by compulsively rubbing the judge's face with a cotton ball dipped in drinking water.

Because of its vastness, the collection will undoubtedly inspire thousands of pages of criticism, praise, and commentary. But its importance is best summarized by Martin himself: "I don't really know too much about art."

REVIEW OF
WINSLOW HOMER SHOW AT
L.A. COUNTY ART MUSEUM

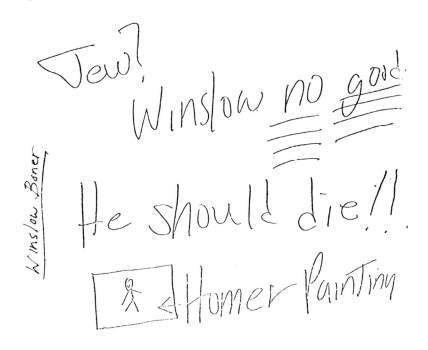

THE DIARRHEA GARDENS OF
EL CAMINO REAL

Outside San Diego, just across from the old mission, there sits a plot of land of particular beauty, the famous Diarrhea Gardens of El Camino Real. The Diarrhea Gardens were founded in 1573 by mission Indians when they first ate the food of the white man. Later, when stuffy missionaries tried to rid the Indians of their customs and traditions, the Diarrhea Gardens were spared because their removal was, to quote Father Serra, "piled high with difficulties."

When the Gardens were rediscovered in 1952, everyone turned conservationist and did their best to preserve the land for the thousands of tourists they knew would flock there. Even Howard Johnson refused to build a hotel on that spot in order to preserve the land. So, as it often is with areas of rare beauty, the Diarrhea Gardens still lie in the shade of the magnolia trees, and still give their aroma to the wafting sea breezes that head up the coast to San Clemente.

TURDS

THE TURDS NEVER BECAME accepted in this
country because of their name. The Turds,
or people from Turdsmania, were people of
healthy stock. They were tall, with long
straight hair; the men robust, the women
bold and beautiful. The first Turds arrived
on these shores in fifteen eighty-nine, one
year after the defeat of the Spanish Armada.
They were unjustly blamed for the defeat of
the Spanish Fleet when a Spanish admiral
remarked, "No wonder we lost, we had a
bunch of turds managing our cannons!"

When finally in America, they also had
trouble with lodgings. Most boarding
houses had a sign on the front, "No Turds."
The Turdsmen naturally interpreted it to

44

mean, "No people from Turdsmania, please." They consequently felt rejected, as would any turd.

Even those who decided to return to Turdsmania had a rough time going back. Once on the boat, they would ask, "Where do the Turds stay?" And a mate would innocently reply, "Why, in the can, sir," thinking it was some kind of Navy test. The Turdsmen would spend the rest of the voyage huddled in the men's room. Once back in the homeland, however, their lot became a happier one. Each man and woman could pass each other on the street and proudly say, "I'm a Turd!"

THE UNDERTAKERS

OLD POPS HAD BEEN stone cold dead for two days. He was rigid, gruesome and had turned slightly green and now he lay on a slab at the undertakers, about to be embalmed by two lovable old morticians.

"At least he lived to a ripe age," said one.

"Yep," said the other. "Well, let's get to 'er."

Suddenly, Old Pops bolted upright and without opening his eyes, began to utter this story:

"In 1743, Captain Rice set sail from England with an unreliable and mutinous crew. After three days at sea, the mast of the mainsail splintered, and then broke completely in half. The ship tossed about at sea for two days; the men mutinied, and the ship tossed about for another two days. At the end of the third day, a ship appeared on the horizon and rescued them and good Captain Rice failed to mention to the admiral the incident of mutiny, and his crew became faithful and hard-working and devoted themselves to their captain."

Old Pops laid back down on the marble.

"Well," said one mortician, "there goes the old saying, 'dead men tell no tales'!"

THE DAY THE DOPES
CAME OVER

I WAS SITTING at home, peeking through the blinds at my neighbor's wife, minding my own business, when my doorbell rang. "Who's there?" I shouted. "We don't know," came the reply. I immediately knew the dopes had come over.

I opened the door and invited them in. I was happy to have company even if they were a bunch of dopes.

"Well, what brings you over this way?" I queried.

"Yup."

"Yup."

"Yup."

"Yup," they said.

"Would you like some coffee?" I asked.

"Gol," said one dope, "how long have we been here?"

"About two minutes."

"Gol, we should have left hours ago!" And they packed up some of my things and lumbered out.

"Goodbye Dopes!" I shouted.

They turned to me and shouted back, "Goodbye, you big fuckin' idiot!"

THE SMOKERS

HE LIT the cigarette and smoked it down to the filter in one breath. He silently thanked the Winston Company for being thoughtful enough about his health to include a filter to protect him. So he lit up another. This time he didn't exhale the squeaky-clean filtered smoke, but just let it nestle in his lungs, filling his body with that good menthol flavor. Some more smokers knocked on his door and they came in and all started smoking along with him.

"How wonderful it is that we're all smoking," he thought.

Everyone smoked and smoked and after they smoked they all talked about smoking and how nice it was that they were all smokers and then they smoked some more.

Smoke, smoke, smoke. They all sang "Smoke That Cigarette" and "Smoke Gets in Your Eyes." Then the smokers smoked one more cigarette and left him alone in his easy chair, about to relax and enjoy a nice quiet smoke. And then his lips fell off.

SHE HAD THE JUGS

YES, SHE WAS WITTY; she was intelligent. She was born of high station. She spoke and walked proudly. She was the kind who displayed nobility, who showed style and class. But above all, *she had the jugs*.

Many people called her by her last name; some closer friends had a confidence with her and shared the intimacy of her first name. But to me, she was always "Lady jugs a-plenty."

It is true. She was clever and she was charming, but above all, *she had the jugs*.

SEX CRAZED
LOVE GODDESSES

LITTLE BILLY JACKSON had to go to the store for his mother to pick up some postage stamps. When he got there, he found the stamp machine to be out of order, and decided to walk the extra three blocks to the post office. On the way there, he passed a hardware store, a variety store and a lamp shop. The line was short at the post office and he got the stamps quickly and returned home. His dog, "Spider," bounded out to greet him as his mom waved from the porch. Billy's mother was pleased at the job he did and congratulated him on having enough sense to go to the post office when he found the stamp machine broken. Billy had a nice dessert that night and went to bed.

WOMEN WITHOUT BONES

THE AMAZON SHELTERED many tribes of people from the civilized world. Among them were the primitive Brazilian river dwellers and the Chinese displaced Mud-standers. But perhaps the most frightening tribe known along the Amazon was the Women Without Bones.

The Women Without Bones (*Humanus de filet*) had been practically disregarded by ethnologists because of their poor posture: Who wanted to spend three years studying a bunch of slouchers? But today their curious habits have attracted many American Nutty-Putty hobbyists into their mysterious wilderness. We can look forward to the day scientists will be able to study the Women

Without Bones and answer such questions as "What time is it?" and "How come no bones?"

THE CHILDREN CALLED HIM BIG NOSE

THE INNOCENT CRUELTY of children is something each of us has to face. Their simple honesty sometimes compliments, but more often hurts us. Each person has to accept the verdict of the children, and know that they are right. For example, a friend of ours is known to the children as "big nose." They refer to him in the most casual manner, "Big nose, pass the butter," or "Thank you for the dolly, big nose!" Although he doesn't show it, I think secretly inside he is hurt by it. The adults, of course, tactfully call him "abundant nose," and even young Thomas just out of high school has the courtesy to call him simply, "The Nose."

O, sometimes I wonder why children

can't be born with an innate sense of re-
spect. But at least one person has learned
something about himself, because *the children called him big nose.*

WRONG NUMBER

ONE DAY I CALLED someone up and got the wrong number. I apologized profusely but then realized just an apology was not enough. I offered some money as partial compensation and then threw in some stocks and bonds at the last minute. Then I thought, perhaps if I could take their address and send them everything I own, then take a journey to Tibet to acquire *wisdom*, I could then inform them of the *truth*, something money cannot buy. Naturally they were still indignant, but were at least convinced of my sincerity in wanting to make it right. They suggested that after I go to Tibet, I kill myself, thus offering my last breath as penance. This seemed slightly out of line, but not being a good businessman, I agreed.

So now I'm in Tibet, standing on my head on a llama, thinking 'bout the day I got dat *wrong number*.

MORSE AND THE
NAUGHTY MAGNETS

ONE MORNING BILL POTTER, the clerk at the Old Sweets Shoppe, awoke to find his toes being sucked on by two Chinese telegraph operators. Unable to communicate with them, he marched down to the Western Union office, the Chinese still sucking on his toes, and spoke with Elmo, the town's telegrapher.

"Elmo, you been having trouble with the telegraph again?"

"Oh, about a month ago we . . ." Elmo noticed the Chinese suckers.

"Elmo, you send any telegrams to China?"

Elmo looked sheepish.

"Well, about five weeks ago, Jack Jarvis

came in here and sent a message up to the railroad camp. Here's a copy of it: 'Sent to Chinese a potter's wheel, good luck.' Maybe the message got a little garbled."

Mr. Potter looked directly at Elmo. "Well, for gosh sakes, send an S-O-S up there for them to come down here and get 'em off me!"

Elmo rushed hurriedly to the machine.

Somewhere up in Wyoming, a telegraph operator and several Chinese were listening to the magic sounds of the telegraph. The telegrapher wrote down the message. "D–O–D . . . D–O–D. . . ."

DYNAMITE KING

THE DYNAMITE FACTORY had worked over-
time for the last year, having produced
enough dynamite to equal one-one hun-
dredth of an atom bomb. Biff stood in the
center of the factory. To his left, the dynamite lay in piles to the ceiling. To his right,
the powder lay in open kegs six rows across.
A gross of caps was exposed in the boxes
before him. Biff paused for a cigarette. He
flicked the match out and tossed it haphaz-
ardly over his shoulder. He took several
puffs off the cigarette before he realized that
he didn't smoke, and tossed the butt to one
side.

Just then, Biff fell asleep. "I must really

be tired," he said to himself as he crumpled to the ground in a heap.

When he woke up four hours later, Biff knew he would have trouble adjusting to all the changes that took place in the world during his sleep. Outside, he could already see strange flying machines with no wings and people walking six feet above the ground. Biff checked at his feet; below him was a stick of dynamite and next to it a match. He picked up the dynamite in his hand and lit it. He figured that the odds of the wick snuffing itself out before the flame reached the powder were one in seven billion. He watched the flame climb rapidly down the wick. Then, in the last moments, the flame snuffed itself out.

"This must be my lucky day!" said Biff. And he walked out into the new world.

THE GIFT OF
THE MAGI INDIAN GIVER

CAROLYN WANTED SO MUCH to give Roger something nice for Christmas, but they didn't have much money, and they had to spend every last cent on candy for the baby. She walked down the icy streets and peered into shop windows.

"Roger is so proud of his shinbones. If only I could find some way to get money to buy shinbone polish."

Just then, a sign caught her eye. "Cuticles bought and sold." Many people had told Carolyn of her beautiful cuticles, and Roger was especially proud of them, but she thought, "This is the way I could buy Roger the shinbone polish!" And she rushed into the store.

Later at home, she waited anxiously as Roger came up the steps of their flat. He opened the door and wobbled over to the fireplace, suspiciously holding one arm behind his back.

"Merry Christmas!" they both said, almost simultaneously.

Roger spoke. "Hey, Nutsy, I got you a little something for Christmas."

"Me too," said Carolyn, and they exchanged packages.

Carolyn hurriedly opened her package, staring in disbelief. "Cuticle Frames?! But Roger, I sold my cuticles so I could afford to buy you some shinbone polish!"

"Shinbone polish!" said Roger, "I sold my shinbones to buy you the cuticle frames!" Roger wobbled over to her.

"Well, I'll be hog-tied," said Carolyn.

"You will? Oh, boy!" said Roger.

And it turned out to be a great Christmas after all.

POODLES . . . GREAT EATING!

THESE DAYS IT'S HARD to look at a poodle without thinking what a great meal he would make. This newest American delicacy, once considered "taboo," is now being enjoyed more and more by the average hamburger-buying housewife, as well as the experienced gourmet.

The dog-eating experience began in Arkansas, August, 1959, when Earl Tauntree, looking for something to do said, "Let's cook the dog." It was from these ethnic beginnings that the "smell of the poodle roasting" captured the upper register of restaurants in New York and Miami. Now, restaurant chefs once reluctant to allow anyone but themselves to select meat are permitting patrons to bring in their own dogs for cooking on the spot. Of course, the big question is, is this just a culinary fad, or has America opened her palates to a new eating discovery that can perhaps give new meaning to the old expression "hot-dog"? No one but time can answer that question, but I tell you one thing, you can save the wishbone for me!

SHUCKIN' THE JIVE

THE CRAZY BASTARDS were going down to the pool hall to play a little pinball when their car exploded blowing everyone to smithereens. Some of Tubby's flesh flew off to the side of the road, and in time nourished a sunflower growing there. Soon the sunflower was eaten by a horse and the horse was eaten by some hobos out for a wild time. Then one of the hobos met an eastward wandering Canadian guru. But before anything significant could happen the hobo died, being attacked by a dog heart in a scientist's laboratory. The death was listed as a heart attack. Then slavery was abolished.

CONCLUSION

Grandpa died and was resurrected after three days, but no one called him the Son of God; they just said, "Hey, that's Gramps!"

HOW TO FOLD SOUP

WE MIDDLE-CLASS FOLKS are now all pretty much aware that the lunchpail is strictly a boorish accoutrement. It's just about impossible to maintain an air of dignity when you're carting around a clumsy tin box with a bologna sandwich in it. Yet, it *is* certainly stylish to bring one's own lunch to work. Many people who sought the *chic* of a brought-from-home lunch weren't about to tote that bulky lunchpail, and the answer for most citizens was to hide the food on their body, then at lunchtime produce it from various pockets and hidden belts. This is a wonderful solution and can even give the most dreary office building a certain outdoorsy feel.

However, with all the ingenuity involved in hiding various delicacies on the body, this process automatically excludes certain foods. For example, a turkey sandwich is welcome, but the cumbersome cantaloupe is not (science has provided some relief, of course, like the pecan-sized watermelon ready to be popped into the mouth). One person lined a pocket with vinyl so he could carry around dip and munch all day, dipping the chips into his vest pocket and having them emerge fully doused with onion spread. Another acquaintance had a sport coat equipped with a banana loader, arranged so that by lowering his arm a banana would secretly drop into his hand. This proved ideal for long meetings that continued through lunch, as the drop was made so discreetly that others would naturally think you had been eating a banana all along.

These "tricks" may seem too elaborate for the average unique person desiring to bring their lunch from home, yet still insisting on a fully-balanced meal. The answer is

soup. Soup is a robust addition to any meal and just about everyone has a favorite. But the primary concern is "how can you carry soup on your body without appearing ridiculous?" When you ask yourself this question, you are ready for soup folding.

SOUP FOLDING

First prepare the soup of your choice and pour it into a bowl. Then, take the bowl and quickly turn it upside down on a cookie tray. Lift the bowl ever so gently so that the soup retains the shape of the bowl. *Gently* is the key word here. Then, with a knife cut the soup down the middle into halves, then quarters, and *gently* reassemble the soup into a cube. Some of the soup will have run off onto the cookie tray. Lift this soup up by the corners and fold slowly into a cylindrical soup staff. Square off the cube by stuffing the cracks with this cylindrical soup staff. Place the little packet in your purse or inside coat pocket, and pack off to work. When that lunch bell chimes, impress your friends by forming the soup back into a bowl shape, and enjoy! Enjoy it until that day when the lunchpail comes back into vogue and we won't need soup folding or cornstalks up the leg.

THE VENGEFUL CURTAIN ROD

THE STORY OF the vengeful curtain rod is an exciting and dramatic tale told by the people who only say "hup hup" on the east coast of Borneo. The real facts are vague and misty, but the legend of the vengeful curtain rod as told by the people who only say "hup hup" goes like this:

"Hup hup hup hup hup hup hup hup hup hup hup."

However, the story of the vengeful curtain rod is found throughout other mythologies. In the Egyptian Book of the Comedians, for example, the subject is conspicuously avoided. It is mentioned profusely, however, in the Dead Sea Scrolls (Stinky MacFarland translation). Even Plato, in his little-known dialogue, "Plenty of Soap," deviated from his topic long enough to discuss "the metaphor of the vengeful curtain rod." And in modern times, T. S. Eliot in his poem, "Good Morning, America, I Love You," cites Stinky's translation of the Dead Sea Scrolls in a footnote.

COWS IN TROUBLE

THESE WERE NOT the average "contented" cows. They were cows born for trouble. They were not cows who could stand by and let people call them "bossy." They were cows who could not hang around all day lowing. They were cows who could be just as happy chewing someone else's cud as their own. These were renegade cows.

My first experience with the renegade cows began one day as I was admiring a particularly attractive cow at Johnson's Weed Farm. As I stood there watching her sultry body moving lithely through the rushes, I noticed several other cows staring at me through the weeds, giving me that look that only a cow can give.

Later that night, I was at home thinking over the day's events. The Rubber Duck Throwing Contest, the parade that followed: bands and floats and baton-tossing girls all marching down the middle of the Missouri River. I *should* have been analyzing the glare of those cows I'd seen earlier that day.

The doorbell rang. I opened the door, glad to have a visitor, but found myself face to face with three renegade cows. I could not see their eyes behind the dark glasses.

They ambled in and I did not try to stop them.

That night they just stood around my bed and watched me sleep, much the same way my potatoes do, and I guess you might say I learned my lesson: *Don't fool with renegade cows.*

THE COMPLETE WORKS OF ALFREDO FRANCESI

ALFREDO FRANCESI WAS a man of few words, and fewer ideas. His works, consequently, are a sequence of rambling sentences that only occasionally find ideas to which to attach themselves. His writing was found by Legs Mahoney to be "deplorable and assinine." Following are the complete works and letters.

Dialogue of four people not talking to each other:

"The phase was incomplete . . ."
"Goons, all goons."
"I feel like a . . . like a . . . Oh, I
"don't know . . ."
"Don't say hi."

Francesi's letters to his wife:

(August 12) Gone to market. Be back
later.

(October 22) Gone to market, be back
soon.

SOCIETY IN ASPEN

ASPEN'S NEWEST CRAZE:
LAZY MAN'S HORSESHOES

THROWING HORSESHOES is a game as old as time itself. There is evidence that early amoebas were playing horseshoes nearly four billion years ago.[1] Modern horseshoes began in Turkey about two million years before Christ (Christ himself played the game with uncanny accuracy), and no doubt was used to settle disputes among tribesmen about who could throw horseshoes the best. The game evolved somewhat oddly: the post first being discovered, then the horseshoe, and finally, the horse.

Today, modern man has revived this ancient pastime, and especially here in As-

1. Journal of Scientific Verbage. "Amoebas Without Morals" P. 271: August, 1972.

84

pen, posts can be seen springing up everywhere. But horseshoes has been cursed with a time-consuming chore: removing the shoes from the horse. The newest innovation in the game, consequently, has been to leave the shoes where they are, and toss the entire animal. This gives the game a new sophistication, introducing breeds and show animals to the playing field. Also, greater skills are required and different throwing styles have emerged: the American, the English, and the Thud. The first two are essentially the same with the exception that in the American, if a tossed horse misses the post, he is kicked in the genitals. The third, the Thud, is a three-quarters-higher toss than the American or English, and derives its name from the sound the animal makes on arrival. However, it's the horse's movement through the air that distinguishes most modern horseshoe players. Some toss the horse so it spins vertically, end over end; others try to keep the airborne horse motionless. In spite of the variances, the object is the same: to rest the horse's foot directly on top of the post.

With the influx of visitors into the Aspen area for horseshoe season, a primer for locals on modern horseshoe technique is necessary. With your left hand, grasp the horse by the nape of the neck, the right hand going under the buttocks. Lift firmly, keeping your eyes on the post before you. Decide whether you want to throw the poor beast laterally or vertically; then build your desire. Desire is the key to winning modern horseshoes. Think of the glory. Think of the firm bulging muscles on the animal you are holding. The statuesque legs, that great build. Then, heave! With proper concentration, and a little practice, the horse will hurtle gracefully toward the goal with astounding precision. Feel the satisfaction, as although this may not be the first case of a rider throwing a horse, it may be one of the most premeditated.

The development of Lazy Man's Horseshoes in Aspen is a hopeful step toward a new sports consciousness in Colorado. With enough support from the community, it is the kind of thing that can put Colorado on the map. So let's get behind the horse, give it a little push, and not be afraid to put both feet into whatever comes out.

THE DAY
THE BUFFALO DANCED

KINGS AND QUEENS had heard of the legend of the dancing buffalo of South Dakota. This story had traveled by word of mouth throughout the world, and today people who were interested in that sort of thing were arriving by the hundreds. Among them could be counted authors, critics, painters, rich industrialists and the usual supply of uninformed gawkers who probably couldn't appreciate something such as this.

The event was taking place on a grass-covered farmland nestled in a rolling valley in South Dakota. In the center of the valley floor was a hand-cranked Victrola. The spectators ringed the hills that surrounded the field. Then a farmer walked disinterestedly to the Victrola, as though he were about to do something he'd done a thousand times before. He cranked up the music box and set the needle down. A kind of Dixieland banjo band sound emerged from the box, almost inaudible at first, and everyone turned in anticipation toward the buffalo.

At first the herd paid little attention to this lively music that was slowly building through the valley. But then a buffalo raised his head toward the crowd, and then toward the music's source. The huge buffalo stared at the Victrola momentarily, then looked at a few of his companions. They eyed each other as though communicating some strange curious thought. One buffalo then walked casually, but deliberately, toward the music. The others hesitated, then followed, at first struggling but then picking up the pace of their leader. As the music built, the buffalo appeared to be listening intently and as the song began to crescendo with the banjos and trombones becoming irresistibly exciting, one buffalo began to sway, at first almost imperceptibly. But then the others joined in; their movement became more and more obvious. Suddenly one buffalo, as though in some sort of mystic celebration, rose up on his hind legs, moving them in a manner reminiscent of an old soft-shoe dancer, his front legs pointing daintily in various directions. Then the other buffalo began rising up, dancing around like vaudevillians, in an incredible climax of sound and motion.

The music ended. The buffalo ceased their delirious dance, some glancing at the music box as they returned to their grazing in a nearby corner of the field.

THINGS NOT TO BE

Don't be a slyboots
Cunning, shrewd, a rogue
Don't be a shyboots,
Nobody likes a slyboots.

Everyone wants to like you
so why be a slowpoke?
Nobody likes slowpokes
Slowpokes lose favor.

Don't you give a reason
to be known as a
ragamuffin
People look down on
ragamuffins
and they'll look down on you
if they can call you one

How would you like to be known as
one who pussyfoots?
Don't be a pussyfooter and stay away
from those who do.

NO MAN'S LAND

No man's land is where I find
my hand sometimes demand for
me to stop! Oh oh she cried
Oh ooh ah ah don't violate me so!

Don't violate me so I cannot tell the
preacher who connected Edgar's
wallet that was found inside the
bedroom doorway with the absence
of his wallet in his pants.

In his pants that love delivered
an emission on a system-conscious social
        debutante!

OH MERCY,
THE PROSE-POEM TRYPTCH!

I

Semblances of spring, I told her, come like
daisies suddenly tumbling winter's sky.
Doves, I said,
are seen in an instant, carelessly glimpsed.
Histories
tell of moments only, ages strung on unseen
slips of
spider's silk. Gifts they are, I said.

II

Melancholy selves tell several relations of
senseless
involvement in things of myself and things
of the past,
and things much less likely than a summer's
rain,
or a gaslamp.

III

"Oh listen! There are poets on the hill!"
Then turn your head toward skyed
    sparrows. Say:
"Poets! lift your arms for us, come in the
    meadowed fields with
limbs of saddened noggins! Tell us of corn,
    of summer, of crowds,
but most of all, tell us of the bouquets inside
    your heads!"

COMEDY EVENTS YOU CAN DO

1) For something funny, sing this to the tune of "Ebb Tide":
   First, the tide rushes in,
   second, it plants a kiss on the shore,
   and third, I've got my heart open wide like the
   sea is open wide, I know it is. Oh, sing it.

2) When at an elegant dinner party, excuse yourself to go to the bathroom. When you return say, "Boy, I really smelled up the place in there."

3) (for men only) Go up to your best friend and say, "I like you, George, but personally I prefer a stronger man."

4) Put an atom bomb in your nose, go to a party and take out a handkerchief. Then pretend to blow your nose, simultaneously triggering the bomb.

5) Go to the Huntington Gallery and hold a razor blade a quarter of an inch away from "The Blue Boy," and shout "Ding dong, ding dong. . . ."

DR. FITZKEE'S
LUCKY ASTROLOGY DIET

THE PROBLEM WITH the diets of today is that most women who do achieve that magic weight, seventy-six pounds, are still fat. Dr. Fitzkee's Lucky Astrology Diet is a sure-fire method of reducing with the added luxury that you *never feel hungry.*

Here's how the diet works:

FOODS ALLOWED

First Month:	One egg
Second Month:	A raisin
Third Month:	Pumpkin pie with whipped cream and chocolate sauce.

If after the third month you haven't gotten to your dream weight, try lopping off parts of your body until those scales tip just right for you.

THE MORNING I
GOT OUT OF BED

IT SEEMED JUST another morning. I woke and thought, "What to do, what to do." Then, and I don't know why this struck me, but I thought, "Perhaps I'll get out of bed." I know it *seems* crazy now, but then I was just in that particular mood where anything seemed reasonable.

I got up quickly, and only later did I stop to consider what I had done. I was proud. Perhaps now I had paved the way for other men, but the most satisfying thought was that perhaps it might be easier for me . . . *next time.*

WHAT TO SAY WHEN
THE DUCKS SHOW UP

I, FOR ONE, am going to know what to say when the ducks show up. I've made a list of phrases, and although I don't know which one to use yet, they are all good enough in case they showed up tomorrow. Many people won't know what to say when the ducks show up, but I will. Maybe I'll say, "Oh ducks, oh ducks, oh ducks," or just "ducks wonderful ducks!" I practice these sayings every day, and even though the ducks haven't come yet, when they do, I'll know what to say.

THE YEAR WINTER
LASTED NINE MINUTES

WELL, WE WERE all set for a long winter. We got the wood out; we got the animals barned up. It was the last of November and we felt winter coming and suddenly we saw the storm start to hit, and it was fierce. We rushed inside and got the fire goin', and Ma started some broth. Then about nine minutes later, it was spring. Dangdest thing I ever saw. There we were, standin' outside in our mufflers an' sheepskin coats, seein' the birds chirpin' and the flowers bloomin' and it was about ninety degrees. Then, we all just looked at each other for about two weeks.

THE ALMADEN SUMMER

LA LA LOO de doo . . . Oh, gawsh . . . Hey, buddy . . . Hey, cumon back . . . la la la la . . . Dime fa a cuwa coffa? Hey . . . la la la.

THE NERVOUS FATHER

"Daddy, where did I come from?"

"Uh . . . uh . . . Well, Tommy, well, it seems . . . well . . . Why, Why out of the garbage can, son. The garbage man comes and throws you in the garbage can and Mommy goes out and gets you. You see, the garbage men pick you up at the creampuff, cherry gingerbread house run by the angels with the puppy faces, and the North Star wonder men with the magic seeds tiptoe 'round the huckleberry tree."

"Well, where did the clock-radio come from?"

"Oh . . . Same place."

DOGS IN MY NOSE

WHEN I WOKE UP that morning, it didn't take me long to realize there were dogs in my nose. I could hear their muffled barks; I could feel their playful vibrations.

It's not dangerous to have dogs in your nose, in fact, it's quite all right to leave them in there for an hour or so. But in this case, because they got in there without permission, I decided to expel them immediately, coaxing them out with a piece of hamburger.

The dogs popped out and landed on the floor. They shook their little floppy ears and bounded off, and I was amused at the prospect of some other weary traveler awakening to find he had *dogs in his nose*.

AWARDS

LAST YEAR at Awards time, two or three people picked most of them up. Their works were indeed superior and the judges had little choice. But this year at Awards time, the men in tuxedos and women in gowns of exotic cloths and laces heard an even, if not odd, distribution of prizes. The administrators at first gave reasons for certain awards, as though making excuses for decisions of which they were once confident.

"The MacFarland award to Mister Falcon because he spent a lot of time summarizing first."

The room was a murmur and Falcon stood up and marched toward the stage and his coat-tails brushed the oak of the walls of this old building.

Then Jackson was given the prize of distinguished accomplishment. The crowd lowly grumbled and a few peripheral members applauded. The judges seemed defiant, as though they were acting on new information.

The judges continued passing awards out to unlikely people, and favorites were acclaimed in categories they never expected.

And so for forty-five minutes the crowd sat astonished and listened to judges announcing awards for stature and flow of the line.

I think that after the first thirty minutes, the members, now mellowed by wine, began to understand and rejoice in the course of the evening and conversation and wit were heard in the room with the dim chandeliers. Then everyone picked up their wraps and awards, walked outside in the light snow, departed in carriages, or some in their cars, and vanished into a black night, thinking of something they knew long ago.

RIVERS OF THE DEAD

THE RIVERS OF THE DEAD is not what you think, but a book lain unopened for seventy years. The printers and binders of the Rivers of the Dead faintly remembered through records of transactions who brought it to them. He was thin and cold.

"We were made to print the pages on paper like vellum, a rough finish, but deep to the touch of the hand. And he acted as though these words were important. The title was finished in gold."

The frontispiece indicated seven copies were made, none sold but given away. The author was listed as Webb.

The language of the book was odd and peculiar, but the ideas were clear, if unfamiliar, when the book was read slowly with care. And, on occasion, the words were rhapsodic and luxurious. It seemed to be an elevation of thought, quite unlike anything written before. There seldom were commas, and no quotations. And the readers of the book were profounded and shaken and they altered their walk and stared away. And all of them mentioned the last chapter was the puzzle. The book was clear till that chapter. It seemed to be either the writer stumbling, or a passage written with extreme eloquence. Now they were trying to decipher the meaning of that last section called the Rivers of the Dead.

NOVEMBER 1

It's so far away you stand
that I wonder
to tell you
by yelling
is less than
poetic my dear

NOVEMBER 5

and I am perhaps that. Again suppose
or perhaps another, well, imagine
    possibility
of, again, assuming thus, or then that which
can be no sooner than he did I, well, go on
(you have, by the way, rather smooth skin).

NOVEMBER 9

Several hours later,
and quite significantly so,
we were quiet; again,
we were quiet,
(more than before)

NOVEMBER 12

lovers lost in phrases
continued to cry
"we shall open, and rise!"
(now I am told,
"we have been set upon,
like a small boy standing in the sea.")

NOVEMBER 16

Oh me oh my
ha ha ha ha
tee hee hee
(I speak to several; I think of you)
rains. "it's good morning
to you." "it's from a long
night last night."
"Do you think it will" rain?

(a voice aches)

NOVEMBER 18

(entered in a journal)

    Thurs. Approx. 2:a.m. I swear I heard her call my name from the street.

NOVEMBER 25

A thread strains to say goodbye
you snip the thread goodbye

THE LAST THING
ON MY MIND

FOR ABOUT TWO DAYS now, I have been trying to figure out what is the last thing on my mind. It's not an easy task because you have to think of all the first things on your mind, then the middle things on your mind, and then there's a lot of false hopes raised as you just think you've thought of it and then suddenly you're thinking of something else. For a while I thought it was "my sister's big toe," but then "ball peen hammer" occurred to me. I was about ready to write that down as the last thing on my mind when "foodelee-doodelee" struck me for some reason, and then in quick succession, "caraway seed," "twelve feet," and "dog pie." But then I realized how stupid I had been.

124

The last thing on my mind was always, "The last thing on my mind." Every time I thought of something, I would check to see if it was "the last thing on my mind." So no matter what I thought of, it was always followed with, "the last thing on my mind." Therefore, according to the law of infinite regression which says it is illegal for anything to repeat infinitely, the last thing on my mind is "the last thing on my mind."

ACKNOWLEDGMENTS

Yakkity yak yak yak yakkity yak yakkity yakkity yak yak yak yak yakkity yak yak yak yakkity.